# "To His Coy Mistress" and Other Poems

## ANDREW MARVELL

DOVER PUBLICATIONS, INC.
Mineola, New York

# DOVER THRIFT EDITIONS

GENERAL EDITOR: STANLEY APPELBAUM
EDITOR OF THIS VOLUME: PAUL NEGRI

## Copyright

Copyright ©1997 by Dover Publications, Inc.
All rights reserved under Pan American and International Copyright Conventions.

Published in Canada by General Publishing Company, Ltd., 30 Lesmill Road, Don Mills, Toronto, Ontario.
Published in the United Kingdom by Constable and Company, Ltd., 3 The Lanchesters, 162–164 Fulham Palace Road, London W6 9ER.

## Bibliographical Note

This Dover edition, first published in 1997, is a new selection of 25 poems reprinted from a standard source. The Note and footnotes have been specially prepared for this edition.

## Library of Congress Cataloging-in-Publication Data

Marvell, Andrew, 1621–1678.
    "To his coy mistress" and other poems / Andrew Marvell.
        p.      cm. — (Dover thrift editions)
    ISBN 0-486-29544-3 (pbk.)
    I. Title.   II. Series.
PR3546.A6    1997
821'.4 — dc21                                                           96-45478
                                                                                    CIP

Manufactured in the United States of America
Dover Publications, Inc., 31 East 2nd Street, Mineola, N.Y. 11501

# Note

IN HIS LIFETIME, Andrew Marvell (1621–1678) was known primarily for his political verse and prose satires and his involvement in the turbulent English politics of the times. The poems on which his reputation rests today, such masterpieces as "To His Coy Mistress," "The Garden" and other love poems and lyrics, were not published until three years after his death and received only scant attention then. While Marvell found favor with some late eighteenth- and nineteenth-century critics and poets (Lamb, Coleridge and Wordsworth among them), it was not until the landmark 1921 publication of Sir Herbert Grierson's *Metaphysical Lyrics and Poems of the Seventeenth Century* and T. S. Eliot's essays on the metaphysical poets that his stature as a major poet was established and a wide general readership achieved.

Marvell was born at Winestead, Yorkshire, near Hull, the son of a Puritan minister. He attended Trinity College, Cambridge, and after graduating traveled extensively in Europe for four years. In 1650 he accepted a position as tutor to the daughter of Sir Thomas Fairfax, the Commonwealth general, and resided at Nun Appleton House in Yorkshire for two years. It was during this period that Marvell wrote most of his love poems and lyrics and his single longest poem, directly inspired by his stay at the Fairfax family seat, "Upon Appleton House." An enthusiastic supporter of Oliver Cromwell, Marvell attained a position in the Cromwell government as Assistant Latin Secretary to John Milton in 1657. (After the Restoration, Marvell defended Milton against charges of regicide and is credited with helping to save him from imprisonment or worse.) After Cromwell's death in 1658, Marvell served as a member of Parliament from Hull. During this time he attacked the Restoration government and the court of Charles II in verse and prose satires and pamphlets until his death in 1678.

This volume includes most of Marvell's love poems, lyrics, religious poems and two major "political" poems, "An Horatian Ode upon Cromwell's Return from Ireland" and "Upon Appleton House." Recurrent themes in these poems include the conflict between carnal and idealized love, between sensuality and spirituality; the contrasting merits of a life of action and participation and those of a contemplative life of withdrawal from worldly affairs; man's relation to nature and his place in the natural world; and other timeless issues that make Marvell so relevant to readers today.

Marvell is considered a metaphysical poet (the school of poetry represented by John Donne and such contemporaries as Herbert, Crashaw, Vaughn and others). Among the characteristics of metaphysical poetry abundantly present in Marvell's work are the use of ingenious metaphors or "conceits"; the witty, often paradoxical tone; a flexible meter and irregular rhythm akin to natural speech; and a striving to see beyond the surface to the essential nature of a subject. Of all the metaphysical poets, Marvell is perhaps the most accessible. While his ideas are complex, his language is generally clear and simple. His arguments can be followed and his observations appreciated without detailed knowledge of the many philosophical and literary traditions on which they often rest. And best of all, the sheer musicality of his language and the direct sensual appeal of his imagery make a reading of his poems a pleasurable experience for any lover of poetry, regardless of his or her level of literary sophistication.

For this edition, spelling has generally been modernized, except where doing so would alter the rhyme or meter. Note also that in poems of this period, the verb ending "-ed" counts as a separate syllable when printed in full, even when this is not the case today. For example: "wingèd" in "Time's wingèd chariot hurrying near" ("To His Coy Mistress," p. 1) is given two syllables. This is shown in the present edition by the accent "è." Punctuation has been altered occasionally to make the meaning plainer. New explanatory footnotes have been provided.

# Contents

# TO HIS COY MISTRESS

Had we but world enough, and time,
This coyness, lady, were no crime.
We would sit down, and think which way
To walk, and pass our long love's day.
Thou by the Indian Ganges' side
Should'st rubies find: I by the tide
Of Humber would complain. I would
Love you ten years before the Flood:
And you should if you please refuse
Till the conversion of the Jews.[1]
My vegetable love should grow
Vaster than empires, and more slow.
An hundred years should go to praise
Thine eyes, and on thy forehead gaze.
Two hundred to adore each breast:
But thirty thousand to the rest.
An age at least to every part,
And the last age should show your heart.
For, lady, you deserve this state;
Nor would I love at lower rate.

But at my back I always hear
Time's wingèd chariot hurrying near:
And yonder all before us lie
Deserts of vast eternity.
Thy beauty shall no more be found;
Nor, in thy marble vault, shall sound
My echoing Song: then worms shall try
That long preserv'd virginity:
And your quaint honor turn to dust,
And into ashes all my lust.
The grave's a fine and private place,
But none I think do there embrace.

Now therefore, while the youthful hue
Sits on thy skin like morning dew,
And while thy willing soul transpires
At every pore with instant fires,
Now let us sport us while we may;
And now, like am'rous birds of prey,
Rather at once our time devour,

---

[1] *conversion of the Jews*: to occur just before the Last Judgment.

Than languish in his slow-chapp'd power.[2]
Let us roll all our strength, and all
Our sweetness, up into one ball:
And tear our pleasures with rough strife,
Thorough the iron gates of life.
Thus, though we cannot make our sun
Stand still, yet we will make him run.

# THE DEFINITION OF LOVE

My love is of a birth as rare
As 'tis for object strange and high:
It was begotten by Despair
Upon Impossibility.

Magnanimous Despair alone
Could show me so divine a thing,
Where feeble Hope could ne'er have flown
But vainly flapp'd its tinsel wing.

And yet I quickly might arrive
Where my extended soul is fix'd,
But Fate does iron wedges drive,
And always crowds itself betwixt.

For Fate with jealous eye does see
Two perfect loves; nor lets them close:
Their union would her ruin be,
And her tyrannic pow'r depose.

And therefore her decrees of steel
Us as the distant poles have plac'd,
(Though love's whole world on us doth wheel)
Not by themselves to be embrac'd,

Unless the giddy heaven fall,
And earth some new convulsion tear;
And, us to join, the world should all
Be cramp'd into a planisphere.[1]

---

[2] *slow-chapp'd power*: the power of slowly moving and devouring jaws.

---

[1] *planisphere*: a hypothetical flat, i.e., two-dimensional, sphere.

As lines so loves oblique may well
Themselves in every angle greet:
But ours so truly parallel,
Though infinite can never meet.

Therefore the love which us doth bind,
But Fate so enviously debars,
Is the conjunction of the mind,
And opposition of the stars.

# THE MOWER TO THE GLOWWORMS

Ye living lamps, by whose dear light
The nightingale does sit so late,
And studying all the summer-night,
Her matchless songs does meditate;

Ye country comets, that portend
No war, nor prince's funeral,
Shining unto no higher end
Than to presage the grass's fall;

Ye glowworms, whose officious flame
To wand'ring mowers shows the way,
That in the night have lost their aim,
And after foolish fires do stray;

Your courteous lights in vain you waste,
Since Juliana here is come,
For she my mind hath so displac'd
That I shall never find my home.

# THE MOWER AGAINST GARDENS

Luxurious[1] man, to bring his vice in use,
  Did after him the world seduce:
And from the fields the flow'rs and plants allure,
  Where Nature was most plain and pure.
He first enclos'd within the garden's square
  A dead and standing pool of air:
And a more luscious earth for them did knead,
  Which stupefi'd them while it fed.
The pink grew then as double as his mind;
  The nutriment did change the kind.
With strange perfumes he did the roses taint,
  And flowers themselves were taught to paint.
The tulip, white, did for complexion seek;
  And learn'd to interline its cheek:
Its onion root they then so high did hold,
  That one was for a meadow sold.
Another world was search'd, through oceans new,
  To find the marvel of Peru.
And yet these rarities might be allow'd,
  To man, that sov'reign thing and proud;
Had he not dealt between the bark and tree,
  Forbidden mixtures there to see.
No plant now knew the stock from which it came;
  He grafts upon the wild the tame:
That the uncertain and adult'rate fruit
  Might put the palate in dispute.
His green seraglio has its eunuchs too;
  Lest any tyrant him outdo.
And in the cherry he does Nature vex,
  To procreate without a sex.
'Tis all enforc'd; the fountain and the grot;
  While the sweet fields do lie forgot:
Where willing Nature does to all dispense
  A wild and fragrant innocence:
And fawns and fairies do the meadows till,
  More by their presence than their skill.
Their statues polish'd by some ancient hand,
  May to adorn the gardens stand:
But howsoe'er the figures do excel,
  The gods themselves with us do dwell.

---

[1] *Luxurious*: voluptuous, lecherous.

# DAMON THE MOWER

Hark how the mower Damon sung,
With love of Juliana stung!
While ev'rything did seem to paint
The scene more fit for his complaint.
Like her fair eyes the day was fair;
But scorching like his am'rous care.
Sharp like his scythe his sorrow was,
And wither'd like his hopes the grass.

"Oh what unusual heats are here,
Which thus our sun-burn'd meadows sear!
The grasshopper its pipe gives o'er;
And hamstring'd frogs can dance no more.
But in the brook the green frog wades;
And grasshoppers seek out the shades.
Only the snake, that kept within,
Now glitters in its second skin.

"This heat the sun could never raise,
Nor Dog-star so inflames the days.
It from an higher beauty grow'th,
Which burns the fields and mower both:
Which made the Dog, and makes the sun
Hotter than his own Phaeton.[1]
Not July causeth these extremes,
But Juliana's scorching beams.

"Tell me where I may pass the fires
Of the hot day, or hot desires.
To what cool cave shall I descend,
Or to what gelid fountain bend?
Alas! I look for ease in vain,
When remedies themselves complain.
No moisture but my tears do rest,
Nor cold but in her icy breast.

---

[1] *Phaeton*: Phaëthon, son of Apollo who came to grief when he drove his father's solar chariot.

"How long wilt thou, fair Shepherdess,
Esteem me, and my presents less?
To thee the harmless snake I bring,
Disarmèd of its teeth and sting.
To thee chameleons changing hue,
And oak leaves tipp'd with honey dew.
Yet thou ungrateful hast not sought
Nor what they are, nor who them brought.

"I am the Mower Damon, known
Through all the meadows I have mown.
On me the morn her dew distills
Before her darling daffodils.
And, if at noon my toil me heat,
The sun himself licks off my sweat.
While, going home, the ev'ning sweet
In cowslip-water bathes my feet.

"What, though the piping shepherd stock
The plains with an unnumber'd flock,
This scythe of mine discovers wide
More ground than all his sheep do hide.
With this the golden fleece I shear
Of all these closes ev'ry year.
And though in wool more poor than they,
Yet am I richer far in hay.

"Nor am I so deform'd to sight,
If in my scythe I lookèd right;
In which I see my picture done,
As in a crescent moon the sun.
The deathless fairies take me oft
To lead them in their dances soft;
And, when I tune myself to sing,
About me they contract their ring.

"How happy might I still have mow'd,
Had not Love here his thistles sow'd!
But now I all the day complain,
Joining my labor to my pain;
And with my scythe cut down the grass,
Yet still my grief is where it was:
But, when the iron blunter grows,
Sighing I whet my scythe and woes."

While thus he threw his elbow round,
Depopulating all the ground,
And, with his whistling scythe, does cut
Each stroke between the earth and root,
The edged steel by careless chance
Did into his own ankle glance;
And there among the grass fell down,
By his own scythe, the mower mown.

"Alas!" said he, "these hurts are slight
To those that die by Love's despite.
With shepherd's purse, and clown's allheal,
The blood I staunch, and wound I seal.
Only for him no cure is found,
Whom Juliana's eyes do wound.
'Tis death alone that this must do:
For, Death, thou art a mower too."


# THE MOWER'S SONG

My mind was once the true survey
Of all these meadows fresh and gay;
And in the greenness of the grass
Did see its hopes as in a glass;
When Juliana came, and she
What I do to the grass, does to my thoughts and me.

But these, while I with sorrow pine,
Grew more luxuriant still and fine;
That not one blade of grass you spi'd,
But had a flower on either side;
When Juliana came, and she
What I do to the grass, does to my thoughts and me.

Unthankful meadows, could you so
A fellowship so true forgo,
And in your gaudy May-games meet,
While I lay trodden under feet?
When Juliana came, and she
What I do to the grass, does to my thoughts and me.

But what you in compassion ought,
Shall now by my revenge be wrought:
And flow'rs, and grass, and I and all,
Will in one common ruin fall.
For Juliana comes, and she
What I do to the grass, does to my thoughts and me.

And thus, ye meadows, which have been
Companions of my thoughts more green,
Shall now the heraldry become
With which I shall adorn my tomb;
For Juliana comes, and she
What I do to the grass, does to my thoughts and me.

## THE UNFORTUNATE LOVER

Alas, how pleasant are their days
With whom the infant Love yet plays!
Sorted by pairs, they still are seen
By fountains cool, and shadows green.
But soon these flames do lose their light,
Like meteors of a summer's night:
Nor can they to that region climb,
To make impression upon time.

'Twas in a shipwreck, when the seas
Rul'd, and the winds did what they please,
That my poor lover floating lay,
And, ere brought forth, was cast away:
Till at the last the master-wave
Upon the rock his mother drave;
And there she split against the stone,
In a Caesarean section.[1]

The sea him lent these bitter tears
Which at his eyes he always bears.
And from the winds the sighs he bore,
Which through his surging breast do roar.

---

[1] Pronounced in three syllables.

No day he saw but that which breaks
Through frighted clouds in forked streaks.
While round the rattling thunder hurl'd,
As at the fun'ral of the world.

While Nature to his birth presents
This masque of quarreling elements,
A num'rous fleet of corm'rants black,
That sail'd insulting o'er the wrack,[2]
Receiv'd into their cruel care
Th' unfortunate and abject heir:
Guardians most fit to entertain
The orphan of the hurricane.

They fed him up with hopes and air,
Which soon digested to despair.
And as one corm'rant fed him, still
Another on his heart did bill.
Thus while they famish him, and feast,
He both consumèd, and increas'd:
And languishèd with doubtful breath,
Th' amphibium of life and death.

And now, when angry heaven would
Behold a spectacle of blood,
Fortune and he are call'd to play
At sharp before it all the day:
And tyrant Love his breast does ply
With all his wing'd artillery,
Whilst he, betwixt the flames and waves,
Like Ajax, the mad tempest braves.

See how he nak'd and fierce does stand,
Cuffing the thunder with one hand;
While with the other he does lock
And grapple with the stubborn rock:
From which he with each wave rebounds,
Torn into flames, and ragg'd with wounds.
And all he says, a lover drest
In his own blood does relish best.

---

[2] *wrack*: wreckage.

This is the only banneret[3]
That ever Love created yet:
Who though, by the malignant stars,
Forcèd to live in storms and wars:
Yet dying leaves a perfume here,
And music within every ear:
And he in story only rules,
In a field sable a lover gules.

# THE GALLERY

Clora, come view my soul, and tell
Whether I have contriv'd it well.
Now all its several lodgings lie
Compos'd into one gallery;
And the great arras-hangings, made
Of various faces, by are laid;
That, for all furniture, you'll find
Only your picture in my mind.

Here thou art painted in the dress
Of an inhuman murderess,
Examining upon our hearts
Thy fertile shop of cruel arts:
Engines more keen than ever yet
Adornèd tyrant's cabinet,
Of which the most tormenting are
Black eyes, red lips, and curlèd hair.

But, on the other side, th' art drawn
Like to Aurora in the dawn;
When in the east she slumb'ring lies,
And stretches out her milky thighs;
While all the morning choir does sing,
And manna falls, and roses spring;
And, at thy feet, the wooing doves
Sit perfecting[1] their harmless loves.

---

[3] *banneret*: a rank of knighthood conferred on the battlefield.

---

[1] Stressed on the first syllable.

Like an enchantress here thou show'st,
Vexing thy restless lover's ghost;
And, by a light obscure, dost rave
Over his entrails, in the cave;
Divining thence, with horrid care,
How long thou shalt continue fair;
And (when inform'd) them throw'st away,
To be the greedy vulture's prey.

But, against that, thou sitt'st afloat
Like Venus in her pearly boat.
The halcyons, calming all that's nigh,
Betwixt the air and water fly.
Or, if some rolling wave appears,
A mass of ambergris it bears.
Nor blows more wind than what may well
Convoy the perfume to the smell.

These pictures and a thousand more,
Of thee, my gallery do store;
In all the forms thou canst invent
Either to please me, or torment:
For thou alone to people me,
Art grown a num'rous colony;
And a collection choicer far
Than or Whitehall's, or Mantua's[2] were.

But, of these pictures and the rest,
That at the entrance likes me best:
Where the same posture, and the look
Remains, with which I first was took.
A tender shepherdess, whose hair
Hangs loosely playing in the air,
Transplanting flow'rs from the green hill,
To crown her head, and bosom fill.

---

[2] *Than or Whitehall's, or Mantua's*: the art collection of Charles I.

## THE FAIR SINGER

To make a final conquest of all me,
Love did compose so sweet an enemy,
In whom both beauties to my death agree,
Joining themselves in fatal harmony;
That while she with her eyes my heart does bind,
She with her voice might captivate my mind.

I could have fled from one but singly fair:
My disentangled soul itself might save,
Breaking the curlèd trammels of her hair.
But how should I avoid to be her slave,
Whose subtle art invisibly can wreathe
My fetters of the very air I breathe?

It had been easy fighting in some plain,
Where victory might hang in equal choice,
But all resistance against her is vain,
Who has th' advantage both of eyes and voice,
And all my forces needs must be undone,
She having gainèd both the wind and sun.

## MOURNING

You, that decipher out the fate
Of human offsprings from the skies,
What mean these infants which of late
Spring from the stars of Chlora's eyes?

Her eyes confus'd, and doublèd o'er,
With tears suspended ere they flow;
Seem bending upwards, to restore
To heaven, whence it came, their woe.

When, molding of the wat'ry spheres,
Slow drops untie themselves away;
As if she, with those precious tears,
Would strow the ground where Strephon lay.

Yet some affirm, pretending art,
Her eyes have so her bosom drown'd,
Only to soften near her heart
A place to fix another wound.

And, while vain pomp does her restrain
Within her solitary bow'r,
She courts herself in am'rous rain,
Herself both Danaë and the show'r.[1]

Nay others, bolder, hence esteem
Joy now so much her master grown,
That whatsoever does but seem
Like grief is from her windows thrown.

Nor that she pays, while she survives,
To her dead love this tribute due;
But casts abroad these donatives,
At the installing of a new.

How wide they dream! The Indian slaves
That sink for pearl through seas profound,
Would find her tears yet deeper waves
And not of one the bottom sound.

I yet my silent judgment keep,
Disputing not what they believe
But sure as oft as women weep,
It is to be suppos'd they grieve.


# AMETAS AND THESTYLIS
# MAKING HAY-ROPES

AMETAS

Think'st thou that this love can stand,
Whilst thou still dost say me nay?
Love unpaid does soon disband:
Love binds love as hay binds hay.

---

[1] *Danaë and the show'r:* Danaë was the daughter of King Acrisius of Argos; Jupiter came to
her in the guise of a golden shower.

THESTYLIS

Think'st thou that this rope would twine
If we both should turn one way?
Where both parties so combine,
Neither love will twist nor hay.

AMETAS

Thus you vain excuses find,
Which yourself and us delay:
And love ties a woman's mind
Looser than with ropes of hay.

THESTYLIS

What you cannot constant hope
Must be taken as you may.

AMETAS

Then let's both lay by our rope,
And go kiss within the hay.

## THE NYMPH COMPLAINING FOR THE DEATH OF HER FAWN

The wanton troopers riding by
Have shot my fawn and it will die.
Ungentle men! They cannot thrive
To kill thee. Thou ne'er didst alive
Them any harm: alas, nor could
Thy death yet do them any good.
I'm sure I never wish'd them ill;
Nor do I for all this; nor will:
But, if my simple pray'rs may yet
Prevail with heaven to forget
Thy murder, I will join my tears
Rather than fail. But, O my fears!
It cannot die so. Heaven's King
Keeps register of everything:
And nothing may we use in vain.
Ev'n beasts must be with justice slain;
Else men are made their deodands.[1]

---

[1] *deodands*: in English law, animals or objects having caused a death and forfeited to the Crown for pious uses.

Though they should wash their guilty hands
In this warm life-blood, which doth part
From thine, and wound me to the heart,
Yet could they not be clean: their stain
Is dy'd in such a purple grain.
There is not such another in
The world, to offer for their sin.

   Unconstant Sylvio, when yet
I had not found him counterfeit,
One morning (I remember well)
Ti'd in this silver chain and bell,
Gave it to me: nay, and I know
What he said then; I'm sure I do.
Said he, look how your huntsman here
Hath taught a fawn to hunt his dear.
But Sylvio soon had me beguil'd.
This waxèd tame, while he grew wild,
And quite regardless of my smart,
Left me his fawn, but took his heart.

   Thenceforth I set myself to play
My solitary time away,
With this: and very well content,
Could so mine idle life have spent.
For it was full of sport; and light
Of foot and heart; and did invite
Me to its game: it seem'd to bless
Itself in me. How could I less
Than love it? O I cannot be
Unkind, t' a beast that loveth me.

   Had it liv'd long, I do not know
Whether it too might have done so
As Sylvio did: his gifts might be
Perhaps as false or more than he.
But I am sure, for ought that I
Could in so short a time espy,
Thy love was far more better than
The love of false and cruel men.

   With sweetest milk, and sugar, first
I it at mine own fingers nurs'd.
And as it grew, so every day
It wax'd more white and sweet than they.
It had so sweet a breath! And oft
I blush'd to see its foot more soft,
And white (shall I say than my hand?),

Nay, any lady's of the land.
    It is a wond'rous thing, how fleet
'Twas on those little silver feet.
With what a pretty skipping grace
It oft would challenge me the race:
And when 't had left me far away,
'Twould stay, and run again, and stay.
For it was nimbler much than hinds;
And trod, as on the four winds.
    I have a garden of my own,
But so with roses overgrown,
And lilies, that you would it guess
To be a little wilderness.
And all the springtime of the year
It only lovèd to be there.
Among the beds of lilies, I
Have sought it oft, where it should lie;
Yet could not, till itself would rise,
Find it, although before mine eyes.
For, in the flaxen lilies' shade,
It like a bank of lilies laid.
Upon the roses it would feed,
Until its lips ev'n seem'd to bleed:
And then to me 'twould boldly trip,
And print those roses on my lip.
But all its chief delight was still
On roses thus itself to fill:
And its pure virgin limbs to fold
In whitest sheets of lilies cold.
Had it liv'd long, it would have been
Lilies without, roses within.
    O help! O help! I see it faint:
And die as calmly as a saint.
See how it weeps. The tears do come
Sad, slowly dropping like a gum.
So weeps the wounded balsam: so
The holy frankincense doth flow.
The brotherless Heliades[2]
Melt in such amber tears as these.
    I in a golden vial will

---

2 *Heliades*: the sisters of Phaëthon; lamenting his death, they were turned into poplar trees, their tears turning to amber.

Keep these two crystal tears, and fill
It till it do o'erflow with mine;
Then place it in Diana's shrine.
  Now my sweet fawn is vanish'd to
Whither the swans and turtles go:
In fair Elysium to endure,
With milk-white lambs, and ermines pure.
O do not run too fast: for I
Will but bespeak thy grave, and die.
  First my unhappy statue shall
Be cut in marble; and withal,
Let it be weeping too: but there
Th' engraver sure his art may spare;
For I so truly thee bemoan,
That I shall weep though I be stone:
Until my tears, still dropping, wear
My breast, themselves engraving there.
There at my feet shalt thou be laid,
Of purest alabaster made:
For I would have thine image be
White as I can, though not as thee.

# DAPHNIS AND CHLOE

Daphnis must from Chloe part:
Now is come the dismal hour
That must all his hopes devour,
All his labor, all his art.

Nature, her own sex's foe,
Long had taught her to be coy:
But she neither knew t' enjoy,
Nor yet let her lover go.

But, with this sad news surpris'd,
Soon she let that niceness fall;
And would gladly yield to all,
So it had his stay compris'd.

Nature so herself does use
To lay by her wonted state,
Lest the world should separate;
Sudden parting closer glues.

He, well read in all the ways
By which men their siege maintain,
Knew not that the fort to gain
Better 'twas the siege to raise.

But he came so full possess'd
With the grief of parting thence,
That he had not so much sense
As to see he might be bless'd.

Till Love in her language breath'd
Words she never spake before;
But then.legacies no more
To a dying man bequeath'd.

For, alas, the time was spent,
Now the latest minute's run
When poor Daphnis is undone,
Between joy and sorrow rent.

At that *Why*, that *Stay my Dear*,
His disorder'd locks he tare;
And with rolling eyes did glare,
And his cruel fate forswear.

As the soul of one scarce dead,
With the shrieks of friends aghast,
Looks distracted back in haste,
And then straight again is fled;

So did wretched Daphnis look,
Frighting her he lovèd most.
At the last, this lover's ghost
Thus his leave resolvèd took.

"Are my hell and heaven join'd
More to torture him that dies?
Could departure not suffice,
But that you must then grow kind?

"Ah, my Chloe, how have I
Such a wretched minute found,
When thy favors should me wound
More than all thy cruelty?

"So to the condemnèd wight
The delicious cup we fill;
And allow him all he will,
For his last and short delight.

"But I will not now begin
Such a debt unto my foe;
Nor to my departure owe
What my presence could not win.

"Absence is too much alone:
Better 'tis to go in peace,
Than my losses to increase
By a late fruition.

"Why should I enrich my fate?
'Tis a vanity to wear,
For my executioner,
Jewels of so high a rate.

"Rather I away will pine
In a manly stubbornness
Than be fatted up express
For the cannibal to dine.

"Whilst this grief does thee disarm,
All th' enjoyment of our love
But the ravishment would prove
Of a body dead while warm.

"And I parting should appear
Like the gourmand Hebrew dead,
While with quails and Manna fed,
He does through the desert err.

"Or the witch that midnight wakes
For the fern, whose magic weed
In one minute casts the seed,
And invisible him makes.

"Gentler times for love are meant;
Who for parting pleasure strain
Gather roses in the rain,
Wet themselves and spoil their scent.

"Farewell therefore all the fruit
Which I could from love receive:
Joy will not with sorrow weave,
Nor will I this grief pollute.

"Fate I come, as dark, as sad,
As thy malice could desire;
Yet bring with me all the fire
That love in his torches had."

At these words away he broke;
As who long has praying li'n,
To his headsman makes the sign,
And receives the parting stroke.

But hence virgins all beware.
Last night he with Phlogis slept;
This night for Dorinda kept;
And but rid to take the air.

Yet he does himself excuse;
Nor indeed without a cause.
For, according to the laws,
Why did Chloe once refuse?

## THE MATCH

Nature had long a treasure made
    Of all her choicest store;
Fearing, when she should be decay'd,
    To beg in vain for more.

Her orientest colors there,
    And essences most pure,
With sweetest perfumes hoarded were,
    All as she thought secure.

She seldom them unlock'd, or us'd,
   But with the nicest care;
For, with one grain of them diffus'd,
   She could the world repair.

But likeness soon together drew
   What she did separate lay;
Of which one perfect beauty grew,
   And that was Celia.

Love wisely had of long foreseen
   That he must once grow old;
And therefore stor'd a magazine,
   To save him from the cold.

He kept the several cells replete
   With nitre thrice refin'd;
The naphta's and the sulphur's heat,
   And all that burns the mind.

He fortifi'd the double gate,
   And rarely thither came;
For, with one spark of these, he straight
   All nature could inflame.

Till, by vicinity so long,
   A nearer way they sought;
And, grown magnetically strong,
   Into each other wrought.

Thus all his fuel did unite
   To make one fire high:
None ever burn'd so hot, so bright;
   And, Celia, that am I.

So we alone the happy rest,
   Whilst all the world is poor,
And have within ourselves possess'd
   All love's and nature's store.

# YOUNG LOVE

Come, little infant, love me now,
  While thine unsuspected years
Clear thine agèd father's brow
  From cold jealousy and fears.

Pretty surely 'twere to see
  By young love old time beguil'd:
While our sportings are as free
  As the nurse's with the child.

Common beauties stay fifteen;
  Such as yours should swifter move;
Whose fair blossoms are too green
  Yet for lust, but not for love.

Love as much the snowy lamb
  Or the wanton kid does prize,
As the lusty bull or ram,
  For his morning sacrifice.

Now then love me: time may take
  Thee before thy time away:
Of this need we'll virtue make,
  And learn love before we may.

So we win of doubtful fate;
  And, if good she to us meant,
We that good shall antedate,
  Or, if ill, that ill prevent.

Thus as kingdoms, frustrating
  Other titles to their crown,
In the cradle crown their king,
  So all foreign claims to drown;

So, to make all rivals vain,
  Now I crown thee with my love:
Crown me with thy love again,
  And we both shall monarchs prove.

# THE PICTURE OF LITTLE T. C.
# IN A PROSPECT OF FLOWERS

See with what simplicity
This nymph begins her golden days!
In the green grass she loves to lie,
And there with her fair aspect tames
The wilder flow'rs, and gives them names:
But only with the roses plays;
          And them does tell
What color best becomes them, and what smell.

Who can foretell for what high cause
This darling of the gods was born!
Yet this is she whose chaster laws
The wanton love shall one day fear,
And, under her command severe,
See his bow broke and ensigns torn.
          Happy, who can
Appease this virtuous enemy of man!

O then let me in time compound,
And parley with those conquering eyes;
Ere they have tri'd their force to wound,
Ere, with their glancing wheels, they drive
In triumph over hearts that strive,
And them that yield but more despise.
          Let me be laid,
Where I may see thy glories from some shade.

Meantime, whilst every verdant thing
Itself does at thy beauty charm,
Reform the errors of the spring;
Make that the tulips may have share
Of sweetness, seeing they are fair;
And roses of their thorns disarm:
          But most procure
That violets may a longer age endure.

But, O young beauty of the woods,
Whom nature courts with fruits and flow'rs,
Gather the flow'rs, but spare the buds;
Lest Flora, angry at thy crime,

To kill her infants in their prime,
Do quickly make th' example yours;
   And, ere we see,
Nip in the blossom all our hopes and thee.


# THE GARDEN

How vainly men themselves amaze
To win the palm, the oak, or bays;[1]
And their incessant labors see
Crown'd from some single herb or tree,
Whose short and narrow verged shade
Does prudently their toils upbraid;
While all flow'rs and all trees do close
To weave the garlands of repose.

Fair Quiet, have I found thee here,
And Innocence, thy sister dear!
Mistaken long, I sought you then
In busy companies of men.
Your sacred plants, if here below,
Only among the plants will grow.
Society is all but rude
To this delicious solitude.

No white nor red was ever seen
So am'rous as this lovely green.
Fond lovers, cruel as their flame,
Cut in these trees their mistress' name.
Little, alas, they know, or heed,
How far these beauties hers exceed!
Fair trees! wheres'e'er your barks I wound,
No name shall but your own be found.

When we have run our passion's heat,
Love hither makes his best retreat.
The gods, that mortal beauty chase,
Still in a tree did end their race.

---

[1] *the palm, the oak, or bays*: awards for athletics, civic service and poetry, respectively.

Apollo hunted Daphne so,
Only that she might laurel grow.
And Pan did after Syrinx speed,
Not as a nymph, but for a reed.

What wond'rous life in this I lead!
Ripe apples drop about my head;
The luscious clusters of the vine
Upon my mouth do crush their wine;
The nectarine and curious peach
Into my hands themselves do reach;
Stumbling on melons, as I pass,
Ensnar'd with flow'rs, I fall on grass.

Meanwhile the mind, from pleasure less,
Withdraws into its happiness:
The mind, that ocean where each kind
Does straight its own resemblance find;
Yet it creates, transcending these,
Far other worlds, and other seas;
Annihilating all that's made
To a green thought in a green shade.

Here at the fountain's sliding foot,
Or at some fruit tree's mossy root,
Casting the body's vest aside,
My soul into the boughs does glide:
There like a bird it sits, and sings,
Then whets and combs its silver wings;
And, till prepar'd for longer flight,
Waves in its plumes the various light.

Such was that happy Garden-state,
While man there walk'd without a mate:
After a place so pure, and sweet,
What other help could yet be meet!
But 'twas beyond a mortal's share
To wander solitary there:
Two paradises 'twere in one
To live in Paradise alone.

How well the skillful gard'ner drew
Of flow'rs and herbs this dial new;
Where from above the milder sun
Does through a fragrant zodiac run;

And, as it works, th' industrious bee
Computes its time as well as we.
How could such sweet and wholesome hours
Be reckon'd but with herbs and flow'rs!


# BERMUDAS

Where the remote Bermudas ride
In th' ocean's bosom unespi'd,
From a small boat, that row'd along,
The list'ning winds receiv'd this song.
  "What should we do but sing his praise
That led us through the wat'ry maze,
Unto an isle so long unknown,
And yet far kinder than our own?
Where he the huge sea-monsters wracks,
That lift the deep upon their backs.
He lands us on a grassy stage;
Safe from the storms and prelates' rage.
He gave us this eternal spring,
Which here enamels everything;
And sends the fowls to us in care,
On daily visits through the air.
He hangs in shades the orange bright,
Like golden lamps in a green night.
And does in the pom'granates close,
Jewels more rich than Ormus[1] shows.
He makes the figs our mouths to meet,
And throws the melons at our feet.
But apples plants of such a price,
No tree could ever bear them twice.
With cedars, chosen by his hand,
From Lebanon, he stores the land.
And makes the hollow seas that roar
Proclaim the ambergris on shore.
He cast (of which we rather boast)
The Gospel's pearl upon our coast,
And in these rocks for us did frame
A temple, where to sound his Name.

---

[1] *Ormus*: Ormuz, or Hormuz, a trading center on the Persian Gulf.

Oh, let our voice his praise exalt,
Till it arrive at heaven's vault:
Which thence (perhaps) rebounding, may
Echo beyond the Mexique Bay."
Thus sung they, in the English boat,
An holy and a cheerful note,
And all the way, to guide their chime,
With falling oars they kept the time.

# A DIALOGUE BETWEEN THE RESOLVÈD SOUL AND CREATED PLEASURE

Courage, my Soul, now learn to wield
The weight of thine immortal shield.
Close on thy head thy helmet bright.
Balance thy sword against the fight.
See where an army, strong as fair,
With silken banners spreads the air.
Now, if thou be'st that thing divine,
In this day's combat let it shine:
And show that nature wants an art
To conquer one resolvèd heart.

PLEASURE

Welcome the creation's guest,
Lord of earth, and Heaven's heir.
Lay aside that warlike crest,
And of nature's banquet share:
Where the souls of fruits and flow'rs
Stand prepar'd to heighten yours.

SOUL

I sup above, and cannot stay
To bait so long upon the way.

PLEASURE

On these downy pillows lie,
Whose soft plumes will thither fly:
On these roses strow'd so plain
Lest one leaf thy side should strain.

SOUL

My gentler rest is on a thought,
Conscious of doing what I ought.

PLEASURE

If thou be'st with perfumes pleas'd,
Such as oft the gods appeas'd,
Thou in fragrant clouds shalt show
Like another god below.

SOUL

A Soul that knows not to presume
Is Heaven's and its own perfume.

PLEASURE

Everything does seem to vie
Which should first attract thine eye:
But since none deserves that grace,
In this crystal view *thy* face.

SOUL

When the Creator's skill is priz'd,
The rest is all but earth disguis'd.

PLEASURE

Hark how music then prepares
For thy stay these charming airs,
Which the posting winds recall,
And suspend the river's fall.

SOUL

Had I but any time to lose,
On this I would it all dispose.
Cease, Tempter. None can chain a mind
Whom this sweet chordage cannot bind.

CHORUS

*Earth cannot show so brave a sight*
*As when a single Soul does fence*
*The batteries of alluring sense,*
*And Heaven views it with delight.*
  *Then persevere: for still new charges sound:*
  *And if thou overcom'st thou shalt be crown'd.*

PLEASURE

All this fair, and soft, and sweet,
    Which scatteringly doth shine,
Shall within one beauty meet,
    And she be only thine.

SOUL

If things of sight such heavens be,
What heavens are those we cannot see?

PLEASURE

Wheresoe'er thy foot shall go
    The minted gold shall lie,
Till thou purchase all below,
    And want new worlds to buy.

SOUL

Wer't not a price who'd value gold?
And that's worth nought that can be sold.

PLEASURE

Wilt thou all the glory have
    That war or peace commend?
Half the world shall be thy slave,
    The other half thy friend.

SOUL

What friends, if to my self untrue?
What slaves, unless I captive you?

PLEASURE

Thou shalt know each hidden cause,
    And see the future time:
Try what depth the center draws,
    And then to Heaven climb.

SOUL

None thither mounts by the degree
Of knowledge, but humility.

CHORUS.

*Triumph, triumph, victorious Soul;*
*The world has not one pleasure more:*
*The rest does lie beyond the pole,*
*And is thine everlasting store.*

# A DIALOGUE BETWEEN THE SOUL AND BODY

SOUL

O who shall from this dungeon raise
A Soul enslav'd so many ways?
With bolts of bones, that fetter'd stands
In feet; and manacled in hands.
Here blinded with an eye; and there
Deaf with the drumming of an ear.
A Soul hung up, as 'twere, in chains
Of nerves, and arteries, and veins.
Tortur'd, besides each other part,
In a vain head, and double heart.

BODY

   O who shall me deliver whole
From bonds of this tyrannic Soul?
Which, stretch'd upright, impales me so,
That mine own precipice I go;
And warms and moves this needless frame:
(A fever could but do the same.)
And, wanting where its spite to try,
Has made me live to let me die.
A body that could never rest,
Since this ill spirit it possess'd.

SOUL

   What magic could me thus confine
Within another's grief to pine?
Where whatsoever it complain,
I feel, that cannot feel, the pain.
And all my care itself employs
That to preserve, which me destroys:
Constrain'd not only to endure
Diseases, but, what's worse, the cure:
And ready oft the port to gain,
Am shipwreck'd into health again.

BODY

   But physic yet could never reach
The maladies thou me dost teach;
Whom first the cramp of hope does tear:
And then the palsy shakes of fear.
The pestilence of love does heat:
Or hatred's hidden ulcer eat.

Joy's cheerful madness does perplex:
Or sorrow's other madness vex.
Which knowledge forces me to know;
And memory will not forgo.
What but a Soul could have the wit
To build me up for sin so fit?
So architects do square and hew
Green trees that in the forest grew.

# ON A DROP OF DEW

See how the orient dew,
Shed from the bosom of the morn
  Into the blowing roses,
Yet careless of its mansion new,
For the clear region where 'twas born
  Round in itself encloses:
  And in its little globe's extent
Frames as it can its native element.
  How it the purple flow'r does slight,
    Scarce touching where it lies,
  But gazing back upon the skies,
    Shines with a mournful light,
      Like its own tear,
Because so long divided from the sphere.
  Restless it rolls and unsecure,
    Trembling lest it grow impure:
  Till the warm sun pity its pain,
And to the skies exhale it back again.
    So the soul, that drop, that ray
Of the clear fountain of eternal day,
Could it within the human flow'r be seen,
    Rememb'ring still its former height,
    Shuns the sweet leaves and blossoms green;
    And, recollecting its own light,
Does, in its pure and circling thoughts, express
The greater heaven in an heaven less.
    In how coy a figure wound,
    Every way it turns away:
    So the world excluding round,
    Yet receiving in the day.
    Dark beneath, but bright above:
    Here disdaining, there in love.

How loose and easy hence to go:
How girt and ready to ascend.
Moving but on a point below,
It all about does upwards bend.
Such did the manna's sacred dew distill;
White, and entire, though congeal'd and chill.
Congeal'd on earth: but does, dissolving, run
Into the glories of th' Almighty Sun.

## EYES AND TEARS

How wisely Nature did decree,
With the same eyes to weep and see!
That, having view'd the object vain,
They might be ready to complain.

And, since the self-deluding sight
In a false angle takes each height,
These tears, which better measure all,
Like wat'ry lines and plummets fall.

Two tears, which sorrow long did weigh
Within the scales of either eye,
And then paid out in equal poise,
Are the true price of all my joys.

What in the world most fair appears,
Yea, even laughter, turns to tears:
And all the jewels which we prize,
Melt in these pendants of the eyes.

I have through every garden been,
Amongst the red, the white, the green;
And yet from all the flow'rs I saw
No honey but these tears could draw.

So the all-seeing sun each day
Distills the world with chemic ray;
But finds the essence only showers,
Which straight in pity back he powers.[1]

---

[1] *powers*: pours.

Yet happy they whom grief doth bless,
That weep the more, and see the less:
And, to preserve their sight more true,
Bathe still their eyes in their own dew.

So Magdalen, in tears more wise
Dissolv'd those captivating eyes,
Whose liquid chains could flowing meet
To fetter her Redeemer's feet.

Not full sails hasting loaden home,
Nor the chaste lady's pregnant womb,
Nor Cynthia teeming shows so fair
As two eyes swoll'n with weeping are.

The sparkling glance that shoots desire,
Drench'd in these waves, does lose its fire.
Yea, oft the Thund'rer pity takes
And here the hissing lightning slakes.

The incense was to Heaven dear,
Not as a perfume, but a tear.
And stars show lovely in the night,
But as they seem the tears of light.

Ope then, mine eyes, your double sluice,
And practice so your noblest use.
For others too can see, or sleep;
But only human eyes can weep.

Now like two clouds dissolving, drop,
And at each tear in distance stop:
Now like two fountains trickle down:
Now like two floods o'erturn and drown.

Thus let your streams o'erflow your springs,
Till eyes and tears be the same things:
And each the other's difference bears;
These weeping eyes, those seeing tears.

# THE CORONET

When for the thorns with which I long, too long,
 With many a piercing wound,
 My Savior's head have crown'd,
I seek with garlands to redress that wrong:
 Through every garden, every mead,
I gather flow'rs (my fruits are only flow'rs),
 Dismantling all the fragrant towers
That once adorn'd my shepherdess's head.
And now when I have summ'd up all my store,
 Thinking (so I myself deceive)
 So rich a chaplet thence to weave
As never yet the King of Glory wore:
 Alas, I find the serpent old
 That, twining in his speckled breast,
 About the flow'rs disguis'd does fold,
 With wreaths of fame and interest.
Ah, foolish man, that would'st debase with them,
And mortal glory, Heaven's diadem!
But thou who only couldst the serpent tame,
Either his slipp'ry knots at once untie,
And disentangle all his winding snare,
Or shatter too with him my curious frame:
And let these wither, so that he may die,
Though set with skill and chosen out with care,
That they, while thou on both their spoils dost tread,
May crown thy feet, that could not crown thy head.

# AN HORATIAN ODE UPON CROMWELL'S RETURN FROM IRELAND

The forward youth that would appear
Must now forsake his muses dear,
 Nor in the shadows sing
 His numbers languishing.
'Tis time to leave the books in dust,
And oil th' unusèd armor's rust,
 Removing from the wall
 The cors'let of the hall.
So restless Cromwell could not cease

In the inglorious arts of peace,
But through advent'rous war
Urgèd his active star.
And, like the three-fork'd lightning, first
Breaking the clouds where it was nurst,
Did thorough his own side
His fiery way divide.
For 'tis all one to courage high
The emulous or enemy;
And with such to enclose
Is more than to oppose.
Then burning through the air he went,
And palaces and temples rent:
And Cæsar's head at last
Did through his laurels blast.
'Tis madness to resist or blame
The force of angry Heaven's flame:
And, if we would speak true,
Much to the man is due
Who, from his private gardens, where
He liv'd reservèd and austere,
As if his highest plot
To plant the bergamot,
Could by industrious valor climb
To ruin the great work of time,
And cast the kingdom old
Into another mold.
Though justice against fate complain,
And plead the ancient rights in vain:
But those do hold or break
As men are strong or weak.
Nature that hateth emptiness,
Allows of penetration less:
And therefore must make room
Where greater spirits come.
What field of all the Civil Wars
Where his were not the deepest scars?
And Hampton[1] shows what part
He had of wiser art.
Where, twining subtle fears with hope,
He wove a net of such a scope,

---

[1] *Hampton*: this line and the several that follow refer to the flight of Charles I from Hampton to Carisbrooke in 1647 and his execution in 1650.

That Charles himself might chase
To Caresbrook's narrow case.
That thence the Royal Actor born
The tragic scaffold might adorn:
   While round the armèd bands
   Did clap their bloody hands.
He nothing common did or mean
Upon that memorable scene:
   But with his keener eye
   The axe's edge did try:
Nor call'd the gods with vulgar spite
To vindicate his helpless right,
   But bow'd his comely head,
   Down as upon a bed.
This was that memorable hour
Which first assur'd the forcèd pow'r.
   So when they did design
   The Capitol's first line,
A bleeding head where they begun
Did fright the architects to run;
   And yet in that the state
   Foresaw its happy fate.
And now the Irish are asham'd
To see themselves in one year tam'd:
   So much one man can do,
   That does both act and know.
They can affirm his praises best,
And have, though overcome, confess'd
   How good he is, how just,
   And fit for highest trust:
Nor yet grown stiffer with command,
But still in the Republic's hand:
   How fit he is to sway
   That can so well obey.
He to the Commons' feet presents
A kingdom, for his first year's rents:
   And, what he may, forbears
   His fame to make it theirs:
And has his sword and spoils ungirt,
To lay them at the public's skirt.
   So when the falcon high
   Falls heavy from the sky,
She, having kill'd, no more does search,
But on the next green bough to perch;

Where, when he first does lure,
    The falc'ner has her sure.
What may not then our Isle presume
While victory his crest does plume!
    What may not others fear
    If thus he crown each year!
A Cæsar he ere long to Gaul,
To Italy an Hannibal,
    And to all states not free
    Shall climacteric be.
The Pict no shelter now shall find
Within his particolored mind;
    But from this valor sad
    Shrink underneath the plaid:
Happy if in the tufted brake
The English hunter him mistake;
    Nor lay his hounds in near
    The Caledonian deer.
But thou the war's and fortune's son
March indefatigably on;
    And for the last effect
    Still keep thy sword erect:
Besides the force it has to fright
The spirits of the shady night,
    The same arts that did gain
    A pow'r must it maintain.


# UPON APPLETON HOUSE

TO MY LORD FAIRFAX[1]

Within this sober frame expect
Work of no foreign architect;
That unto caves the quarries drew,
And forests did to pastures hew;
Who of his great design in pain
Did for a model vault his brain,

Whose columns should so high be rais'd
To arch the brows that on them gaz'd.

---

[1] Marvell resided for two years at Nun Appleton House, the family seat of Sir Thomas Fairfax, as tutor to Fairfax's daughter Mary.

Why should of all things man unrul'd
Such unproportion'd dwellings build?
The beasts are by their dens express'd,
And birds contrive an equal nest;
The low-roof'd tortoises do dwell
In cases fit of tortoise-shell:
No creature loves an empty space;
Their bodies measure out their place.

But he, superfluously spread,
Demands more room alive than dead,
And in his hollow palace goes
Where winds as he themselves may lose.
What need of all this marble crust
T' impark the wanton mote of dust,
That thinks by breadth the world t' unite
Though the first builders fail'd in height?

But all things are composèd here
Like Nature, orderly and near:
In which we the dimensions find
Of that more sober age and mind,
When larger-sizèd men did stoop
To enter at a narrow loop;
As practicing, in doors so strait,
To strain themselves through Heaven's gate.

And surely when the after age
Shall hither come in pilgrimage,
These sacred places to adore,
By Vere and Fairfax[2] trod before,
Men will dispute how their extent
Within such dwarfish confines went,
And some will smile at this, as well
As Romulus his bee-like cell.

Humility alone designs
Those short but admirable lines,
By which, ungirt and unconstrain'd,
Things greater are in less contain'd.

---

[2] *Vere and Fairfax*: Thomas Fairfax married Anne Vere in 1637.

Let others vainly strive t' immure
The circle in the quadrature!
These holy mathematics can
In ev'ry figure equal man.

Yet thus the laden house does sweat,
And scarce endures the master great:
But where he comes the swelling hall
Stirs, and the square grows spherical;
More by his magnitude distress'd,
Than he is by its straitness press'd;
And too officiously it slights
That in itself which him delights.

So honor better lowness bears
Than that unwonted greatness wears.
Height with a certain grace does bend,
But low things clownishly ascend.
And yet what needs there here excuse,
Where ev'rything does answer use?
Where neatness nothing can condemn,
Nor pride invent what to contemn?

A stately frontispiece of poor
Adorns without the open door:
Nor less the rooms within commends
Daily new furniture of friends.
The house was built upon the place
Only as for a mark of grace;
And for an inn to entertain
Its lord a while, but not remain.

Him Bishops-Hill, or Denton may,
Or Bilbrough, better hold than they,[3]
But Nature here hath been so free
As if she said "leave this to me."
Art would more neatly have defac'd
What she had laid so sweetly waste;
In fragrant gardens, shady woods,
Deep meadows, and transparent floods.

---

[3] *Bishops-Hill, Denton, Bilbrough*: other properties owned by Fairfax.

While with slow eyes we these survey,
And on each pleasant footstep stay,
We opportunely may relate
The progress of this house's fate.
A nunnery first gave it birth;
For virgin buildings oft brought forth.
And all that neighbor-ruin shows
The quarries whence this dwelling rose.

Near to this gloomy cloister's gates
There dwelt the blooming virgin Thwaites;[4]
Fair beyond measure, and an heir
Which might deformity make fair.
And oft she spent the summer suns
Discoursing with the subtle nuns.
Whence in these words one to her weav'd
(As 'twere by chance) thoughts long conceiv'd.

"Within this holy leisure we
Live innocently as you see.
These walls restrain the world without,
But hedge our liberty about.
These bars enclose that wider den
Of those wild creatures callèd men.
The cloister outward shuts its gates,
And, from us, locks on them the grates.

"Here we, in shining armor white,
Like virgin Amazons do fight.
And our chaste lamps we hourly trim,
Lest the great Bridegroom[5] find them dim.
Our orient breaths perfumèd are
With incense of incessant pray'r.
And holy water of our tears
Most strangely our complexion clears.

"Not tears of grief; but such as those
With which calm pleasure overflows;
Or pity, when we look on you

---

[4] *Thwaites*: Isabele Thwaites, Thomas Fairfax's great-great-grandmother. This stanza and those that follow relate the story of her courtship by William Fairfax. She had been placed in the Cistercian convent at Appleton by her guardian to prevent the union.
[5] *Bridegroom*: Christ.

That live without this happy vow.
How should we grieve that must be seen
Each one a spouse, and each a queen;
And can in Heaven hence behold
Our brighter robes and crowns of gold?

"When we have prayèd all our beads,
Some one the holy legend reads;
While all the rest with needles paint
The face and graces of the saint.
But what the linen can't receive
They in their lives do interweave.
This work the saints best represents;
That serves for altar's ornaments.

"But much it to our work would add
If here your hand, your face we had:
By it we would Our Lady touch;
Yet thus she you resembles much.
Some of your features, as we sew'd,
Through ev'ry shrine should be bestow'd.
And in one beauty we would take
Enough a thousand saints to make.

"And (for I dare not quench the fire
That me does for your good inspire)
'Twere sacrilege a man t' admit
To holy things, for Heaven fit.
I see the angels in a crown
On you the lilies show'ring down:
And round about you glory breaks,
That something more than human speaks.

"All beauty, when at such a height,
Is so already consecrate.
Fairfax, I know; and long ere this
Have mark'd the youth, and what he is.
But can he such a rival seem
For whom you Heav'n should disesteem?
Ah, no! and 'twould more honor prove
He your devoto[5a] were than love.

---

[5a] *devoto*: devotee.

"Here live belovèd and obey'd:
　Each one your sister, each your maid.
　And, if our rule seem strictly penn'd,
　The rule itself to you shall bend.
　Our abbess too, now far in age,
　Doth your succession near presage.
　How soft the yoke on us would lie,
　Might such fair hands as yours it tie!

"Your voice, the sweetest of the choir,
　Shall draw Heav'n nearer, raise us higher.
　And your example, if our head,
　Will soon us to perfection lead.
　Those virtues to us all so dear
　Will straight grow sanctity when here:
　And that, once sprung, increase so fast
　Till miracles it work at last.

"Nor is our order yet so nice,
　Delight to banish as a vice.
　Here pleasure piety doth meet;
　One perfecting the other sweet.
　So through the mortal fruit we boil
　The sugar's uncorrupting oil:
　And that which perish'd while we pull
　Is thus preservèd clear and full.

"For such indeed are all our arts;
　Still handling Nature's finest parts.
　Flow'rs dress the altars; for the clothes,
　The sea-born amber we compose;
　Balms for the griev'd we draw, and pastes
　We mold, as baits for curious tastes.
　What need is here of man? unless
　These as sweet sins we should confess.

"Each night among us to your side
　Appoint a fresh and virgin bride;
　Whom if Our Lord at midnight find,
　Yet neither should be left behind.
　Where you may lie as chaste in bed
　As pearls together billeted.
　All night embracing arm in arm,
　Like crystal pure with cotton warm.

"But what is this to all the store
Of joys you see, and may make more!
Try but a while, if you be wise:
The trial neither costs, nor ties."
Now, Fairfax, seek her promis'd faith:
Religion that dispensèd hath;
Which she henceforward does begin;
The nun's smooth tongue has suck'd her in.

Oft, though he knew it was in vain,
Yet would he valiantly complain.
"Is this that sanctity so great,
An art by which you fineli'r cheat?
Hypocrite witches, hence avaunt,
Who though in prison yet enchant!
Death only can such thieves make fast,
As rob though in the dungeon cast.

"Were there but, when this house was made,
One stone that a just hand had laid,
It must have fall'n upon her head
Who first thee from thy faith misled.
And yet, how well soever meant,
With them 'twould soon grow fraudulent:
For like themselves they alter all,
And vice infects the very wall.

"But sure those buildings last not long,
Founded by folly, kept by wrong.
I know what fruit their gardens yield,
When they it think by night conceal'd.
Fly from their vices. 'Tis thy state,
Not thee, that they would consecrate.
Fly from their ruin. How I fear
Though guiltless lest thou perish there."

What should he do? He would respect
Religion, but not right neglect:
For first religion taught him right,
And dazzlèd not but clear'd his sight.
Sometimes resolv'd his sword he draws,
But reverenceth then the laws:
For justice still that courage led;
First from a judge, then soldier bred.

Small honor would be in the storm.
The court him grants the lawful form,
Which licens'd either peace or force
To hinder the unjust divorce.
Yet still the nuns his right debarr'd,
Standing upon their holy guard.
Ill-counsel'd women, do you know
Whom you resist, or what you do?

Is not this he whose offspring fierce
Shall fight through all the universe;
And with successive valor try
France, Poland, either Germany;
Till one, as long since prophesi'd,
His horse through conquer'd Britain ride?
Yet, against fate, his spouse they kept,
And the great race would intercept.

Some to the breach against their foes
Their wooden saints in vain oppose.
Another bolder stands at push
With their old holy-water brush.
While the disjointed abbess threads
The jingling chain-shot of her beads.
But their loud'st cannon were their lungs,
And sharpest weapons were their tongues.

But, waving these aside like flies,
Young Fairfax through the wall does rise.
Then th' unfrequented vault appear'd,
And superstitions vainly fear'd.
The relics false were set to view;
Only the jewels there were true.
But truly bright and holy Thwaites
That weeping at the altar waits.

But the glad youth away her bears,
And to the nuns bequeaths her tears:
Who guiltily their prize bemoan,
Like Gypsies that a child hath stol'n.
Thenceforth (as when th' enchantment ends
The castle vanishes or rends)
The wasting cloister with the rest
Was in one instant dispossess'd.

At the demolishing, this seat
To Fairfax fell as by escheat.[6]
And what both nuns and founders will'd
'Tis likely better thus fulfill'd.
For if the virgin prov'd not theirs,
The cloister yet remainèd hers.
Though many a nun there made her vow,
'Twas no religious house till now.

From that bless'd bed the hero[7] came,
Whom France and Poland yet does fame:
Who, when retirèd here to peace,
His warlike studies could not cease;
But laid these gardens out in sport
In the just figure of a fort;
And with five bastions it did fence,
As aiming one for ev'ry sense.

When in the east the morning ray
Hangs out the colors of the day,
The bee through these known alleys hums,
Beating the dian[7a] with its drums.
Then flow'rs their drowsy eyelids raise,
Their silken ensigns each displays,
And dries its pan yet dank with dew,
And fills its flask with odors new.

These, as their governor goes by,
In fragrant volleys they let fly;
And to salute their governess
Again as great a charge they press:
None for the virgin nymph;[8] for she
Seems with the flow'rs a flow'r to be.
And think so still! though not compare
With breath so sweet, or cheek so fair.

Well shot, ye firemen! Oh, how sweet
And round your equal fires do meet;
Whose shrill report no ear can tell,

---

[6] *escheat*: forfeiture of property to the lord of the manor.
[7] *hero*: Thomas Fairfax.
[7a] *dian*: reveille.
[8] *virgin nymph*: Mary Fairfax.

But echoes to the eye and smell.
See how the flow'rs, as at parade,
Under their colors stand display'd:
Each regiment in order grows,
That of the tulip, pink and rose.

But when the vigilant patrol
Of stars walks round about the pole,
Their leaves, that to the stalks are curl'd,
Seem to their staves the ensigns furl'd.
Then in some flow'r's beloved hut
Each bee as sentinel is shut;
And sleeps so too: but, if once stirr'd,
She runs you through, or asks the word.

Oh thou, that dear and happy isle
The garden of the world ere while,
Thou paradise of four seas,
Which Heaven planted us to please,
But, to exclude the world, did guard
With wat'ry if not flaming sword;
What luckless apple did we taste,
To make us mortal, and thee waste?

Unhappy! shall we never more
That sweet militia restore,
When gardens only had their tow'rs,
And all the garrisons were flow'rs,
When roses only arms might bear,
And men did rosy garlands wear?
Tulips, in several colors barr'd,
Were then the Switzers[9] of our guard.

The gard'ner had the soldier's place,
And his more gentle forts did trace.
The nursery of all things green
Was then the only magazine.
The winter quarters were the stoves,
Where he the tender plants removes.
But war all this doth overgrow:
We ord'nance, plant and powder sow.

---

[9] *Switzers*: Vatican Swiss Guard.

And yet there walks one on the sod
Who, had it pleasèd him and God,
Might once have made our gardens spring
Fresh as his own and flourishing.
But he preferr'd to the Cinque Ports[10]
These five imaginary forts:
And, in those half-dry trenches, spann'd
Pow'r which the ocean might command.

For he did, with his utmost skill,
Ambition weed, but conscience till.
Conscience, that Heaven-nursèd plant,
Which most our earthly gardens want.
A prickling leaf it bears, and such
As that which shrinks at ev'ry touch;
But flow'rs eternal, and divine,
That in the crowns of saints do shine.

The sight does from these bastions ply,
Th' invisible artillery;
And at proud Cawood Castle seems
To point the battery of its beams.
As if it quarrel'd in the seat
Th' ambition of its prelate great.
But o'er the meads below it plays,
Or innocently seems to gaze.

And now to the abyss I pass
Of that unfathomable grass,
Where men like grasshoppers appear,
But grasshoppers are giants there:
They, in their squeaking laugh, contemn
Us as we walk more low than them:
And, from the precipices tall
Of the green spir's, to us do call.

To see men through this meadow dive,
We wonder how they rise alive.
As, under water, none does know
Whether he fall through it or go.
But, as the mariners that sound

---

[10] *Cinque Ports*: a group of five towns important for English naval defense.

And show upon their lead the ground,
They bring up flow'rs so to be seen,
And prove they've at the bottom been.

No scene that turns with engines strange
Does oft'ner than these meadows change.
For when the sun the grass hath vext,
The tawny mowers enter next;
Who seem like Israelites to be,
Walking on foot through a green sea.
To them the grassy deeps divide,
And crowd a lane to either side.

With whistling scythe, and elbow strong,
These massacre the grass along:
While one, unknowing, carves the rail,
Whose yet unfeather'd quills her fail.
The edge all bloody from its breast
He draws, and does his stroke detest;
Fearing the flesh untimely mow'd
To him a fate as black forebode.

But bloody Thestylis, that waits
To bring the mowing camp their cates,
Greedy as kites has truss'd it up,
And forthwith means on it to sup:
When on another quick she lights,
And cries, he call'd us Israelites;
But now, to make his saying true,
Rails rain for quails, for manna dew.

Unhappy birds! what does it boot
To build below the grass's root;
When lowness is unsafe as height,
And chance o'ertakes what scapeth spite?
And now your orphan parents' call
Sounds your untimely funeral.
Death-trumpets creak in such a note,
And 'tis the sourdine[11] in their throat.

---

[11] *sourdine*: a low-sounding trumpet.

Or sooner hatch or higher build:
The mower now commands the field;
In whose new traverse seemeth wrought
A camp of battle newly fought:
Where, as the meads with hay, the plain
Lies quilted o'er with bodies slain:
The women that with forks it fling,
Do represent the pillaging.

And now the careless victors play,
Dancing the triumphs of the hay;
Where every mower's wholesome heat
Smells like an Alexander's sweat.
Their females fragrant as the mead
Which they in fairy circles tread:
When at their dance's end they kiss,
Their new-made hay not sweeter is.

When after this 'tis pil'd in cocks,
Like a calm sea it shows the rocks:
We wond'ring in the river near
How boats among them safely steer.
Or, like the desert Memphis sand,
Short pyramids of hay do stand.
And such the Roman camps do rise
In hills for soldiers' obsequies.

This scene again withdrawing brings
A new and empty face of things;
A level'd space, as smooth and plain,
As clothes for Lely[12] stretch'd to stain.
The world when first created sure
Was such a table rasc and pure.
Or rather such is the toril[13]
Ere the bulls enter at Madril.[14]

For to this naked equal flat,
Which levellers take pattern at,
The villagers in common chase
Their cattle, which it closer rase;

---

[12] *Lely*: a noted English cloth dyer.
[13] *toril*: bullring.
[14] *Madril*: Madrid.

And what below the scythe increast
Is pinch'd yet nearer by the beast.
Such, in the painted world, appear'd
Davenant with th' universal herd.[15]

They seem within the polish'd grass
A landscape drawn in looking glass,
And shrunk in the huge pasture show
As spots, so shap'd, on faces do.
Such fleas, ere they approach the eye,
In multiplying glasses lie.
They feed so wide, so slowly move,
As constellations do above.

Then, to conclude these pleasant acts,
Denton sets ope its cataracts,
And makes the meadow truly be
(What it but seem'd before) a sea.
For, jealous of its Lord's long stay,
It tries t' invite him thus away.
The river in itself is drown'd,
And isles th' astonish'd cattle round.

Let others tell the paradox,
How eels now bellow in the ox;
How horses at their tails do kick,
Turn'd as they hang to leeches quick;
How boats can over bridges sail,
And fishes do the stables scale.
How salmons trespassing are found;
And pikes are taken in the pound.

But I, retiring from the flood,
Take sanctuary in the wood;
And, while it lasts, my self embark
In this yet green, yet growing ark;
Where the first carpenter might best
Fit timber for his keel have press'd,
And where all creatures might have shares,
Although in armies, not in pairs.

---

[15] *Davenant with th' universal herd*: the reference is to a painting of the Six Days of Creation.

The double wood of ancient stocks
Link'd in so thick an union locks,
It like two pedigrees appears,
On one hand Fairfax, th' other Veres:
Of whom though many fell in war,
Yet more to Heaven shooting are:
And, as they Nature's cradle deck'd,
Will in green age her hearse expect.

When first the eye this forest sees
It seems indeed as wood not trees:
As if their neighborhood so old
To one great trunk them all did mold.
There the huge bulk takes place, as meant
To thrust up a fifth element;
And stretches still so closely wedg'd
As if the night within were hedg'd.

Dark all without it knits; within
It opens passable and thin;
And in as loose an order grows,
As the Corinthean porticoes.
The arching boughs unite between
The columns of the temple green;
And underneath the wingèd choirs
Echo about their tunèd fires.

The nightingale does here make choice
To sing the trials of her voice.
Low shrubs she sits in, and adorns
With music high the squatted thorns.
But highest oaks stoop down to hear,
And list'ning elders prick the ear.
The thorn, lest it should hurt her, draws
Within the skin its shrunken claws.

But I have for my music found
A sadder, yet more pleasing sound:
The stock-doves, whose fair necks are grac'd
With nuptial rings, their ensigns chaste;
Yet always, for some cause unknown,
Sad pair unto the elms they moan.
O why should such a couple mourn,
That in so equal flames do burn!

Then as I careless on the bed
Of gelid[16] strawberries do tread,
And through the hazels thick espy
The hatching throstle's shining eye,
The heron from the ash's top
The eldest of its young lets drop,
As if it stork-like did pretend
That tribute to its Lord to send.

But most the hewel's wonders are,
Who here has the holt-felster's[17] care.
He walks still upright from the root,
Meas'ring the timber with his foot;
And all the way, to keep it clean,
Doth from the bark the wood-moths glean.
He, with his beak, examines well
Which fit to stand and which to fell.

The good he numbers up, and hacks;
As if he mark'd them with the ax.
But where he, tinkling with his beak,
Does find the hollow oak to speak,
That for his building he designs,
And through the tainted side he mines.
Who could have thought the tallest oak
Should fall by such a feeble stroke!

Nor would it, had the tree not fed
A traitor-worm, within it bred.
(As first our flesh corrupt within
Tempts impotent and bashful sin.)
And yet that worm triumphs not long,
But serves to feed the hewel's young.
While the oak seems to fall content,
Viewing the treason's punishment.

Thus I, easy philosopher,
Among the birds and trees confer:
And little now to make me, wants
Or of the fowls, or of the plants.
Give me but wings as they, and I

---

[16] *gelid*: cold, frosty.
[17] *hewel*: woodpecker; *holt-felster's*: woodcutter's.

Straight floating on the air shall fly:
Or turn me but, and you shall see
I was but an inverted tree.

Already I begin to call
In their most learned original:
And where I language want, my signs
The bird upon the bough divines;
And more attentive there doth sit
Than if she were with lime-twigs knit.
No leaf does tremble in the wind
Which I returning cannot find.

Out of these scatter'd Sibyl's leaves
Strange prophecies my fancy weaves:
And in one history consumes,
Like Mexique paintings, all the plumes.
What Rome, Greece, Palestine, ere said
I in this light mosaic read.
Thrice happy he who, not mistook,
Hath read in Nature's mystic book.

And see how chance's better wit
Could with a mask my studies hit!
The oak-leaves me embroider all,
Between which caterpillars crawl:
And ivy, with familiar trails,
Me licks, and clasps, and curls, and hales.
Under this antic cope I move
Like some great prelate of the grove.

Then, languishing with ease, I toss
On pallets swoll'n of velvet moss;
While the wind, cooling through the boughs,
Flatters with air my panting brows.
Thanks for my rest, ye mossy banks,
And unto you cool Zephyrs, thanks,
Who, as my hair, my thoughts too shed,
And winnow from the chaff my head.

How safe, methinks, and strong, behind
These trees have I encamp'd my mind;
Where beauty, aiming at the heart,
Bends in some tree its useless dart;

And where the world no certain shot
Can make, or me it toucheth not.
But I on it securely play,
And gall its horsemen all the day.

Bind me, ye woodbines, in your twines,
Curl me about, ye gadding vines,
And oh so close your circles lace,
That I may never leave this place:
But, lest your fetters prove too weak,
Ere I your silken bondage break,
Do you, O brambles, chain me too,
And courteous briars, nail me through.

Here in the morning tie my chain,
Where the two woods have made a lane;
While, like a guard on either side,
The trees before their Lord divide;
This, like a long and equal thread,
Betwixt two labyrinths does lead.
But, where the floods did lately drown,
There at the ev'ning stake me down.

For now the waves are fall'n and dri'd,
And now the meadows fresher dy'd;
Whose grass, with moister color dash'd,
Seems as green silks but newly wash'd.
No serpent new nor crocodile
Remains behind our little Nile;
Unless itself you will mistake,
Among these meads the only snake.

See in what wanton harmless folds
It ev'rywhere the meadow holds;
And its yet muddy back doth lick,
Till as a crystal mirror slick,
Where all things gaze themselves, and doubt
If they be in it or without.
And for his shade which therein shines,
Narcissus-like, the sun too pines.

Oh what a pleasure 'tis to hedge
My temples here with heavy sedge;
Abandoning my lazy side,
Stretch'd as a bank unto the tide;

Or to suspend my sliding foot
On the osier's underminèd root,
And in its branches tough to hang,
While at my lines the fishes twang!

But now away my hooks, my quills,
And angles, idle utensils.
The young Maria[18] walks tonight:
Hide, trifling youth, thy pleasures slight.
'Twere shame that such judicious eyes
Should with such toys a man surprise;
She that already is the law
Of all her sex, her age's awe.

See how loose Nature, in respect
To her, itself doth recollect;
And everything so whisht and fine,
Starts forthwith to its bonne mine.[19]
The sun himself, of her aware,
Seems to descend with greater care;
And lest she see him go to bed,
In blushing clouds conceals his head.

So when the shadows laid asleep
From underneath these banks do creep,
And on the river as it flows
With eben shuts[20] begin to close;
The modest halcyon comes in sight,
Flying betwixt the day and night;
And such an horror calm and dumb,
Admiring Nature does benumb.

The viscous air, wheres'ere she fly,
Follows and sucks her azure dye;
The jellying stream compacts below,
If it might fix her shadow so;
The stupid fishes hang, as plain
As flies in crystal overta'en;
And men the silent scene assist,
Charm'd with the sapphire-wingèd mist.

---

[18] *young Maria*: Mary Fairfax.
[19] *whisht*: silent, hushed; *bonne mine*: good appearance.
[20] *eben shuts*: ebony shutters.

Maria such, and so doth hush
The world, and through the ev'ning rush.
No new-born comet such a train
Draws through the sky, nor star new-slain.
For straight those giddy rockets fail,
Which from the putrid earth exhale,
But by her flames, in Heaven tri'd,
Nature is wholly vitrifi'd.

'Tis she that to these gardens gave
That wondrous beauty which they have;
She straightness on the woods bestows;
To her the Meadow sweetness owes;
Nothing could make the river be
So crystal-pure but only she;
She yet more pure, sweet, straight, and fair,
Than gardens, woods, meads, rivers are.

Therefore what first she on them spent,
They gratefully again present.
The meadow carpets where to tread;
The garden flow'rs to crown her head;
And for a glass the limpid brook,
Where she may all her beauties look;
But, since she would not have them seen,
The wood about her draws a screen.

For she, to higher beauties rais'd,
Disdains to be for lesser prais'd.
She counts her beauty to converse
In all the languages as hers;
Nor yet in those herself employs
But for the wisdom, not the noise;
Nor yet that wisdom would affect,
But as 'tis Heaven's dialect.

Blest nymph! that couldst so soon prevent
Those trains by youth against thee meant;
Tears (wat'ry shot that pierce the mind);
And sighs (love's cannon charg'd with wind);

True praise (that breaks through all defence);
And feign'd complying innocence;
But knowing where this ambush lay,
She scap'd the safe, but roughest way.

This 'tis to have been from the first
In a domestic Heaven nurst,
Under the discipline severe
Of Fairfax, and the starry Vere;
Where not one object can come nigh
But pure, and spotless as the eye;
And goodness doth itself entail
On females, if there want a male.

Go now, fond sex, that on your face
Do all your useless study place,
Nor once at vice your brows dare knit
Lest the smooth forehead wrinkled sit:
Yet your own face shall at you grin,
Thorough the black-bag of your skin;
When knowledge only could have fill'd
And virtue all those furrows till'd.

Hence she with graces more divine
Supplies beyond her sex the line;
And, like a sprig of mistletoe,
On the Fairfacian oak does grow;
Whence, for some universal good,
The priest shall cut the sacred bud;
While her glad parents most rejoice,
And make their destiny their choice.

Meantime, ye fields, springs, bushes, flow'rs,
Where yet she leads her studious hours
(Till fate her worthily translates,
And find a Fairfax for our Thwaites),
Employ the means you have by her,
And in your kind yourselves prefer;
That, as all virgins she precedes,
So you all woods, streams, gardens, meads.

For you Thessalian Tempe's seat
Shall now be scorn'd as obsolete;
Aranjuez, as less, disdain'd;
The Bel-Retiro as constrain'd;[21]
But name not the Idalian Grove,
For 'twas the seat of wanton love;
Much less the dead's Elysian Fields,
Yet nor to them your beauty yields.

'Tis not, what once it was, the world,
But a rude heap together hurl'd;
All negligently overthrown,
Gulfs, deserts, precipices, stone.
Your lesser world contains the same.
But in more decent order tame;
You Heaven's center, nature's lap,
And paradise's only map.

But now the salmon-fishers moist
Their leathern boats begin to hoist;
And, like Antipodes in shoes,
Have shod their heads in their canoes.
How tortoise-like, but not so slow,
These rational amphibii go?
Let 's in: for the dark hemisphere
Does now like one of them appear.

---

[21] *Thessalian Tempe, Aranjuez, Bel-Retiro*: famous gardens.